T0147307

GENEVA EVANS

iUniverse, Inc.
Bloomington

From Agony to Grace

iUniverse books may be ordered through booksellers or by contacting:

iUniverse
1663 Liberty Drive
Bloomington, IN 47403
www.iuniverse.com
1-800-Authors (1-800-288-4677)

ISBN: 978-1-4502-3941-7 (sc)
ISBN: 978-1-4502-3942-4 (hc)
ISBN: 978-1-4502-3943-1 (e)

Printed in the United States of America

iUniverse rev. date: 6/22/12

INTRODUCTION

From Agony to Grace is a story about the life of a little girl who loved to jump rope and play with her dolls, but who never had a chance to dream of what she could become. From early adolescence to adulthood, her life was torn apart by physical abuse, sexual abuse and drug addiction. Her life became a complete train wreck until one day the miraculous happened… she met Jesus!

FOREWORD

Raw. Searing. Penetrating. Compelling. Painful. honest. These are just a few words that describe this autobiographical work written by Geneva Evans.

With unbridled candor, this Christian women gives the world a glimpse into her dark past, her redemption, and her very bright future.

We are extremely proud of Geneva and her bold choice to expose her scars, fears, and disappointments as well as acknowledge her steady recovery. She exemplifies the courage of a lioness that leaves the throng in search of something for which to feed the pride.

Unafraid to take on even the most ferocious predator~ that of tackling her personal demons~ Geneva, the lioness, has tread upon tough terrain and launched out into deep waters for the benefit of many.

We would like to thank Geneva for heeding the Holy Spirit and the words of the Old Testament prophet, Habakkuk, who said, "write the vision and make it plain, so that those who read it may run..."

Millions will read *"From Agony to Grace"* and be prompted to relinquish old, destructive habits. Millions more~globally ~ will hear and read of this women's story, have a greater understanding of others' pain and, hence, be inspired to move to a higher place in life and in God.

For those who perhaps have a jaundiced eye towards those who've been cast and tormented as *"the least of these, "*we strongly urge you to read this story. It will change and challenge your life, filling you with a greater degree of compassion.

We both proudly endorse and highly recommend this book!

*~Bishop Donald and Pastor Phyllis Thompson Hilliard Cathedral International * Perth Amboy, NJ*

This is a story that will stay on your mind long after you've closed the book Geneva's determination is an inspiration to us all. Surely God can do anything!

Dr. B. Glover

This is a compelling real story that will keep you thanking God for every area of your life and even wherever you are right now in your life.

From Agony to Grace solidifies and confirms that we are in the right place and in the right house of God under the right prophet of God, preaching & teaching that God is love and his word is true. Right on my sister and free the readers as you have already been free from your bondage. Remember you are perfectly and wonderfully made and the plans God has for you are unfolding right before us!

May God continue to bless you my sister!

Deacon Juana Bacchus

Dear Geneva

Thank God for transparency and willingness to share, so that someone else can be encouraged and helped by your story. Keep on writing, keep on talking, and keep on serving the Lord. Thank you for being a living testimony of the transforming power of our Lord and Savior, Jesus Christ. Who knew that placing a order for lunch, can lead to a wonderful friendship.

We Love you

"Run Forest, Run !"

Carrie and Manny O

ACKNOWLEDGEMENTS

- I first give honor to my God, who really is the head of my life and who pressed upon me to write this book. I give this book back to God; and, I hope that He is well pleased.

- I thank my mother, who gave birth to me. She could have aborted me, but did not. Thank you, Mom.

- My three children, Tarrence, Kisha, and Calvin Evans, I love all of you so very much. Mommy is sorry for the past and the pain I put you through. I was not there for you, because I allowed what happened to me take me down a 25-

year death row of drug abuse. But, this madness ends with me! *It is over!!!!*

I speak this truth over the lives of my children and the lives of my grandchildren in the name of Jesus!

- I Thank Bishop Donald Hilliard, Jr., for pouring the Word of God into my life each week. This was a blessing to me, even when times were very dark in my life. You always encouraged me, even when you joked about my ponytail or other hairstyles! I know you were always trying to bless me. Thank you!! I want you to know that you are my spiritual father. I look to you as a father figure, as well, for the one I didn't have in my life. Thank you for teaching me how to live holy for God through His Word. You are one of the caring person I have ever met. Who gives his all to his people, who wants more for them then they want for their selves. May God continue to Bless you richly.

- Pastor Phyllis Hilliard, whom I consider my mentor, thank you for inspiring and encouraging me to *"write the journey."* You kept inquiring of me, *"Geneva, how's your book coming along?"* For this I thank you! There were many days I wanted to give up, but I didn't. You allowed me to cry to you and always extended a listening ear. You are one of a kind, a classy lady of virtue who has much wisdom to give to the sisterhood. You are my inspiration for completing this book.

- Pastor Denise Reid

Thank You for telling me about Jesus, and bringing me to the Cathedral International Church. You have been a blessing to me as well as my family.

Thank you for teaching me about healthy relationships. You are powerful women of God who cares about people. You inter act with the Families, and help them to mend relationships. You show us what love really is by your actions toward us. You truly care about us and our families. I still have the gift you gave me the recovery bible when I came to the church. It is a little worn, but I treasure it because it was from you. Thank You Pastor for all your tough Love. It made me a women of God today. With love and gratitude Thank You!

- Deacon Silvia Hare

Thank you for your love you have always shown me you always smile, and treat me with Love thank you for the editing of this book!

- Deacon Brenda Woods

Thank you for the editing of this book, you where the other set of eyes I needed. You have always been there for me when I really needed you. Thank You, Thank you!

- Deacon Alex and Ann Wallace * Shampoo 11 Perth Amboy NJ

  Thank you for all your kindness you and your wife have showed me over the years and all the hair styles!

- Deacon Gerri Johnson

  Thank you for your kind contribution to this project. Thank You!

  J S Photography Linda Pace* Creative Director

  862-215-8459 (mobile) 732- 599-4202 (customer service) Thank You!

I would like to thank my Cathedral International Church Family for all your help.

I Love You!!

MY FAMILY BACKGROUND

•

FOLLOWING GOD AFAR OFF

I was born into a family of nine children – five girls and four boys. I was the one most people referred to as the *"knee baby,"* the one born next to the last child. I remember my father being a sharp dresser and having pearly white teeth. I also remember our family spending all day in church on Sunday. We would leave in the morning and return home when it was dark. My father loved his children and I remember him telling me how smart I was. I felt safe when my father was home or when he used to carry me. Unfortunately, that's all I can remember about my father from my childhood because he left when I was very young. As I began researching my own personal history to write this book, my sister informed me that our father was a deacon in the church, but that he followed the Lord at a distance.

My mother used to cook all the time. Cooking is her passion; I got my love for cooking from her. I can remember my mother feeding the winos that would show up at her back door. She would cook for people almost everyday. If somebody was sick or had death in their family, my mother would prepare meals for them. She was good at assisting others during their times of need. I remember sitting on a stool in the kitchen as my mother would teach all her children how to cook. Every one of us can handle our business in a kitchen!

> Don't follow God afar off. You MUST have a relationship with Him.
> You must read God's Word and know it for yourself! Check the Bible. If it's not in there, then don't believe everything that is preached to you.

When we were a family and our father was at home, we had peace. Then one day, my parents' Bishop died. After his burial, they remained at the gravesite waiting for him to rise on the third day. When he didn't, my father burned his deacon's robe. My father was so busy trying to please man – his bishop – until he really did not know who God was. When his bishop didn't rise on the third day, he got frustrated, left the church, and never went back. Let me 'fast forward' for a moment. When I became a Christian and began attending church regularly, I listened intently to the teachings of my bishop. I also began to read the scriptures for myself. I've often heard my bishop say in his messages that *"the Bible is always right!"*

He would emphasize this. You cannot believe that your pastor is God. He is God's *mouthpiece* to bring His word into our lives and help shape our character. But, my parents got it twisted; they thought their bishop was God. However, they found out later that he was merely a man of flesh, because when he died, he remained dead. Unlike Jesus, he did not rise on the third day.

CHANGE IN OUR HOUSEHOLD

My father began to drink and spend all his money on alcohol and in the bar. When he came home, he had no money for food. Finally, my mother got tired of him wasting his paycheck. Back then, women were not allowed in the bars; it was against the law. If a woman was seen or caught in a bar, she was arrested and taken to jail. One day, my mother went into the bar and knocked my father off the barstool and took the rest of the money he had in his pocket. When she was about to leave, the cops put her in their car. She told them she had kids at home waiting to be fed and if they locked her up, then they had better go feed them!

My mother was fearless. So, the officers let my mother come home to us. After that, my dad began to stay out more and more. My mother left my father and moved to the projects in Newark, New Jersey. She would go to the second-hand stores to get us clothing. We never complained because my mother kept us clean. Mom would say, *"you're not dressed until you're greased."* That meant, you had to have Vaseline® on your face. She would also shine our shoes with it!

I believe my mother lost all hope in God when my father left her with all her children to raise alone. My mother started drinking and hosting card parties at our home. Men began to stay all night playing cards. My sisters, brothers and I used to peek out of our rooms to see all those people in our house. My mother was a beer drinker; she could drink a case in a day!

When mom wasn't able to care for us, my oldest sister would get us ready for school. She used to love making my hair pretty because I would sit still and let her do it. My other sisters cried and complained that it hurt. She would have to fight with them to comb their hair. We never really had a chance to go outside and play because my mother always told us to clean up the house. By the time we finished, the streetlights were on. When it was dark outside, she wouldn't let us go out. If we caught her in a good mood, she would say, *"Alright! Be back before the streetlights come on*!" If we didn't come back home before the streetlights came on, a beating with an iron cord was a certain punishment. She would warn us by saying, *"I'm not beating any clothes!," and* then would wait until we got in the bathtub to carry out her mission. That was so painful. My sister got used to the beatings. She would stay out with her boyfriend, come home when she got ready and just took the beating. Then, mom started beating everybody when one of us did something wrong. I got tired of getting hit for something I did not do. Sometimes, she would not say anything when you did something wrong. She would wait and when she was beating one of us, we'd hear her say, "*Come here! I owe you one, too!*" I really think my mother was releasing her pain out on her children. I truly believe my mother loved her children. She was never nurtured, so she couldn't nurture her own children. In terms of emotional and social health, it's hard for someone to give what they never had. I look back over my life and I say my mother did the best she could with what she had. There wasn't much to work with.

THE FIRST RAPE

Mom met a woman and her husband who started coming over our house to drink, play music and party. We used to watch my mother and her friends dance and get drunk. At that time, I was nine years old. Then one day, I was the only child at home in the house. My sister and brothers were outside. My mother's male friend was going to the store to get some beer. They knew he wasn't going to come right back, so they suggested I go along, thinking that with me around, he'd make his purchase and come right back. So I went with him. We went to the liquor store and he came back to the car. While he was driving, he went down this dark street, stopped the car and parked. Then he started feeling me up. I was scared and I told him to stop, but he didn't. Then it happened; he raped me. As he raped me, I cried and asked God to make him stop, but he didn't. I felt like I was going to die inside. I felt worthless and scared as though it was my fault. My mind began to race and I thought my heart was going to pump out of my chest. I pleaded with this grown man, *"Please stop! You're hurting me!"* I remember a car's headlights shining as it was going by. He got off me with his mouth smelling like a garbage can. I tried to fight him but he was too big to fight; I was only nine years old. I told him I was going to tell my daddy. That's when he said he would tell my mother. He knew how my mother beat us. I was afraid of my mother so I never told her. She didn't play. My mother would beat you if she thought you did something. As he drove up to the house, he said, *"Clean your face up or I'm telling your mother what you did in the car."* I was so scared. We came back from the store and I went upstairs to my room, which I shared with my sisters. I was so angry, I tore off my doll's head. I never told anyone what happened to me in that car.

My sister, who was one year older than me, was raped earlier by my step-brother. When she told my mother, my mother told her to stop lying; she didn't believe my sister. Mom was not the kind of mother you could go to and tell her anything because in the end, it would be your fault. One day, my sister and I were downtown and found forty dollars in the street. We spent the money on some shoes before we came home. Mom did not believe us. That was the worst beating my sister and I ever got. My mother insisted that 'some man' gave the money to us. I believe she was mad because we didn't bring the money home. Things like this let me know I couldn't tell my mother that my innocence had been stolen from me.

MY EMOTIONS CHANGED

> Parents, if you see a change in your child's behavior, you may want to **talk** to them, not yell. Get into their world

I became very angry at my mother, my father, and at God. No one was there to protect me. I started getting in trouble at school. I fought and was often suspended. My sister knew that this behavior was out of character for me. She kept asking me, *"What's the matter,"* but I could not bring myself to tell her what that man had done to me in the car on that dark street. I felt like I was useless. I felt so dirty. Not enough baths could make me feel clean. I felt worthless and angry. I really believed it was my fault that I was raped.

My life began to go downhill. Nobody was paying attention to me. I would play with my dolls and stay in my room when I knew that man was in the house. My mother was drunk and she didn't know what was going on. At least, I want to believe that she didn't. I would put a chair against the door to my room. My sisters used to go out and stay late. Their boyfriends would climb in the window and they would let them in from outside. One night, my mother caught one of my sister's boyfriends coming down the stairs to open the door to let my sisters in. My mother beat everybody in the house – including me – and I had been home with *her*! That's when I promised God that I would never hit my children. I hit my sons just once in their lives.

THE NEW MAN

After awhile, my mother met another man and he moved in the house with us. He was married and he pushed her drinking more. He always came to our house with bags full of groceries, plus a case of beer and liquor. One day, he was going to the ice cream parlor to get ice cream and he said *"Come on, Geneva. Go with me."* I said no. My mother then told me to go with him. It was my birthday and he wanted to buy me ice cream. I went and started feeling the same way in my stomach that I felt when I was raped. So many years later, I realize it really was the Holy Spirit warning me, but

I did not know then what the Holy Spirit was.

I started crying and he asked what was wrong with me. *"We're only going to the store!"* Fortunately, that's all we did and we came back. I didn't know he was going to get me another time. He built my trust and took me places. I began to trust him; I went everywhere with him. I even looked up to him as a father. Then, it happened. He used to take turns taking us to the airport. One night, I was in the truck with him by myself coming back from the airport. He said he had to stop for something. He pulled over, got out, went to the trunk and came back. When he got back in the truck, he put a knife to my neck and told me that if I didn't do what he said, he would kill my mother.

By this time, I was twelve years old. I began to think that it was alright for these men to have their way with me. To this very day, I have an issue with trust. It's hard for me to trust people, particularly men in my house when I'm alone. If it's the cable man, I leave the door open. I am just afraid to be in the house alone with a man.

When I got back home, I tried to tell my mother that this man said he was going to kill her and she said to me, *"Whatever happens in this house stays in this house!"* I went into the closet of my bedroom and began to cry. I really felt that I was cursed or something. *"Am I really my mother's daughter? Why does this keep happening to me?"* I questioned myself out loud.

I felt safe when I went in the closet because it was dark. This way, no one could see me, so nothing could happen to me in there. This time, the pain was much greater than before. I felt like killing myself. I started looking around the house to see how I could take my life. I looked at some rat poison and then I started crying. I just could not go through with it. Then, I thought about cutting my wrist, but I could not do that either. I often wondered why I didn't end my life. Something in me just would not allow me to do it. I was hurting so much inside, that I began to hate *me*. I felt that if I were dead, then I would not have to endure all this pain. *When would it all stop? God, why are you allowing this to happen to me? Why? Why? Why? What did I do? Please, do not let this happen to me again! Please stop the pain I'm feeling inside. I feel like I am on a roller coaster and I'm on it backwards, being pushed back and forth. Please, stop it, please!*

I had made up my mind that I was no longer going to be a good little girl anymore because bad things kept happening to me, although I was good. I started hanging out at my friend's house; her mother was never home. She went to church at night, so I stayed with them and my mother didn't care. I started drinking. When her mother left for church, we would start drinking. I did not like the way it made me feel. The room would spin around and the bed would not stop going around. I threw up all over the place. *"This is supposed to be fun? I don't think so."* I decided never to drink anymore. I didn't like this! My friend's mother came home early from church and she saw her daughter drunk. After that, she never allowed us to stay in her house alone anymore. My friend's mother asked where we got the liquor and my friend told her she got it from her brother, who stole it from his father.

After that, she took us to church with her every time she went. I started singing in the choir with her two daughters. I really felt like I was in heaven when I went to church. I was at peace that everything was going to be alright. Then reality set in. I had to go home; ; back to that hellhole you call home. I would get up early so I would not be left alone in the house with my mother's boyfriend. I would make sure I left with my sisters. But, I came home from school first and I was scared to come home because I knew my mother's boyfriend would find a way to get me home by myself. This went on for years. My older sisters had left home. They were on drugs and alcohol out in the streets.

THE NEW BOYFRIEND

At the age of sixteen, I started hanging out with the wrong crew. I meet this girl who was older than me. She was in the 12th grade, and I was in the 10th.

> If anyone touches you and you say "no," tell them "No means 'no!' If he continues, tell someone. This is called "***rape!***

She introduced me to this guy who was older than me. Wow! My first boyfriend! I was crazy about him; but, when I look back on it, he was an alcoholic. I never smelled his breath without it reeking of liquor. He had me in the bars with him, getting drunk on a school night. Then my boyfriend tried to sleep with me and I told him 'no.' He said he wasn't going to rush me and that he'd wait until I was ready to have sex. I knew you weren't supposed to have relations before marriage, which is why I told him no. When we went to church, I remember hearing the preacher say so. He said it was a sin to sleep with anyone other than your husband or wife. I remembered that. We went on for months with him trying to persuade me to go to bed with him, but I kept saying no. Then one night, he told me he was not taking me home until I had sex with him. He took me down by the railroad track and raped me. Listen: "No" means *'no.'* I realize that now, but at the time, I felt powerless to defend myself.

I went home and my mother asked me where I had been. I lied and told her that I had been at church. She said that I was not at any church at three o'clock in the morning. (Mom saw right through that lie.) She told me I couldn't go outside for three months. I thought about it and decided that I was not going to be in the house for three months and have her boyfriend violate me again. I left home and moved in with my friend who was older than me. We started hanging out and I started working in the bar. They never asked me for any identification because I was so big for my age. I could pass for twenty-one easily at that time. Plus, they thought I was of age because I would come in to the bar with my boyfriend. I know you're wondering what happened to my boyfriend. Well, I dumped him after he raped me.

I eventually dropped out of school, which I really didn't want to do. But I knew my mother would find me at school. I was a smart young lady and always earned good grades. When it came to survival, I did not have many choices in the matter, so I chose to work in the bar where I met all kinds of people, some crazy and some nice. I felt it would be better for me to work than stay home and be abused sexually and physically.

I met another guy. However, I didn't know he was married. We moved in together and I later had my first son. I stopped working in the bar for about a year. After that year, my boyfriend left and went back to his wife. I lost my apartment and I gave my oldest son to my mother. She would not allow me to stay there with them, so I found my friend and she let me stay with her. She told me about a job at another bar. I applied for the job and got it. She later told me about this hairdresser down the street and how fine he was. So, I started going down there to get my hair done. I saw him checking me out, but I would not pay him any attention.

Although he was very handsome, he was old enough to be my father.

Back then, if you were less than fine, you could not get a conversation out of us. A guy had to be nice-looking, have nice hair and a chiseled physique or we wouldn't give him the time of day. I didn't know then that the ones who are not so good-looking were the real catch. They had possibilities and a plan on how they were going to better their life. We would look past them and go for the better-looking guys.

PHYSICAL ABUSE

One particular Thursday, I went to get my hair done. That's when he began talking to me. I was sixteen and this man was 38 years old! He started calling when I was at work and he asked what I was doing after work, and I always had plans to go out with my friends and hang out late until the next morning.

> If, or when, a 38 year old man is interested in you at age 16, drop everything and ***run!!!***

I think at that time, I was looking for a father figure; that's probably why I turned to him. I went to get my hair done one night and I was the last client in the shop. We started drinking and I had too much. I ended up going home with him that night. Then things began to change. I was with him for six months before I moved in with him.

Different girls would call the house and I would question him about this. Then he would hit me. The first time it happened, I forgave him. Then it started happening more and more. For any little thing, he would hit me. If someone made him angry, he would take it out on me, either verbally or physically.

DRUG ADDICTION

This man, who was old enough to be my father, old enough to know better *and* do better, introduced me to cocaine. Instead of refusing, I messed around and developed a habit. Then he would take my paycheck and tell me these bills needed to be paid, so I would leave and go to the clubs and "After Hours" joints. Days would go by and I would come back and he would be glad to see me. One particular night when I went back, he became angry and hit me in the head with a cane. I woke up in the hospital scared. I didn't remember what happened. I knew he'd hit me, but that's all I could remember. I had to get 250 stitches in my head. They were going to release me from the hospital, but I had no where to go, so I went home to my mother. I was there for two days, but I left because her boyfriend came in the room to get me. By this time, I had learned some street smarts and I had a knife under my pillow. When he came in the room this time, I pulled that knife on him. My mother heard the commotion and came in the room. I was trying to tell her that "this dog" was trying to get in my underwear. She asked me to leave, and told me that I was making too much noise and starting trouble.

DAUGHTER IS BORN

•

RETURN TO AN ABUSIVE BOYFRIEND

I left my mother's house and went back to the guy who beat me up. I had nowhere else to go. My friend had left home and was staying with her boyfriend.

My boyfriend was nice for about three months. He was afraid I was going to press charges against him. He took good care of me with the cocaine and alcohol. I found out I was pregnant again. He told me to get an abortion, but I didn't. I stopped drinking and told him that I didn't want to live this way anymore. I stopped getting high until my daughter was born.

Once again, we had nowhere to go because my boyfriend was mad. When my daughter was born, my oldest sister found me at the hospital and asked me to come live with her. However, she neglected to tell me was that she was behind in her rent. I didn't have any money because I was not working at the time. I had stopped when I got pregnant with my daughter. There was no heat in the apartment, which was situated over a bar. I eventually started working there; and, of course, needed child-care for my new baby. I asked my daughter's father if we could come there to stay. He said no. So I called my daughter's godmother and asked her to take care of my baby. I told her that we had no heat in the apartment and I couldn't provide for my child at that time. I knew that with her, my daughter would be somewhere warm and dry, rather than in the streets with me. Unfortunately, I could not properly nurture and care for my daughter. I credit my daughter's godmother with raising her. My addiction worsened, I was getting high more frequently and was strung out on cocaine.

One night, I wanted some drugs, so I called my daughter's father who used to beat me up and I moved back in with him. *(Was I a glutton for punishment, or what?)* He told me to find a job. I started looking for work, had been out all day, was tired, and then couldn't get in the house. Frustrated, I went in the bar that I used to live above with my sister and landed a job there. My boyfriend was at the barbershop working. I had had a few drinks at the bar this particular day. Then I went to the shop to wait for him to close for the day. We were all drunk. For whatever reason, some guy said something smart to me and I cussed at him. Then he hit me. My boyfriend did nothing in my defense. This man tore my blouse in the front and I picked up a straight razor and cut him! I think all that rage and anger that was boiling inside me erupted on this man. *"Oh, my God! God, please help me! I didn't mean to cut this man! Please Lord, help me!"* He kept coming towards me and hit me again. *"I am so sorry! Please, Lord, help me!"* Just one split second and I had lost it. I felt so bad that I could hurt someone like that. The rum and Coke mixed with cocaine had a major part in what happened. You can control your actions, but the drugs and alcohol will control you.

I thought I had killed that man. I was so scared, I ran. Then two days later, the police were looking for me for aggravated assault. I went and found a friend of mine, who happened to be on the police force, and

I turned myself in. He looked at me and asked, *"What happened? You're a nice girl. He must have done something to you."* Somehow, this officer saw the good in me when I didn't see it in myself. I was told later that I came within one inch of killing that guy. I went to jail for aggravated assault for one day. Then my friend (the cop) posted my bail. That no- good man of mine left me there. The court found me "not guilty" because the guy told on himself and got smart with the judge. He admitted to beating me before I cut him. Even when my life was in such turmoil, God had His hand on me. I was so afraid, but He watched over me when I didn't even know Him.

My life was getting worse and worse. I got fired from the bar because the owner heard about the incident at the barbershop. I went to another bar seeking a job where my mother was working in the kitchen.

I asked her not to tell my age so I could get the job, since I was turning eighteen in two days, anyway. The law had just been passed that you could drink in the bar at age 18 instead of 21. I would work, take my tips, go to the "after hours," and get high all night. At daybreak, I would go home, shower, and go back to work. I had a friend who worked and got high with me. We were on a path of self-destruction together! Then she started dealing for the mob. I let her go as a friend; that was just too risky for me. They were looking for her one day because she had been reported missing. Flyers were out with her pictures on them. She was eventually found in a pipe drain with a plastic bag over her head. This poor woman had been shot in the head and left for dead. They said she had been alive for some time, but the rats had badly eaten her body. Even then, God was looking out for me because it could have been me down in that drain with this woman.

As time progressed, my mother and I were back on good terms again as mother and daughter. One day, she said to me *"You can come home. I'm there by myself anyway."*

DEATH OF MY BROTHER

Everything was going very well at my mother's house for about a month. Then, one day the phone rang. I answered it; my sister was on the other end. It was an emergency; someone had killed my brother. He had been given some poisoned drugs and was lying dead in a hallway. That was a horrible time for the family. We had to bring all the family members in for his funeral. In spite of the sad occasion, it felt good to see the family together. Everyone was so caring. I really missed my brother. He used to come home with something for us every Friday. When he didn't, he'd tell us to iron his clothes and he'd give us five dollars. His clothes did not need ironing; he had just gotten them out of the cleaners. However, we got the money anyway. Although he was our step-brother, we loved him just the same. We found out about him as we got older.

After the funeral, everyone went back to where they lived and my mother's boyfriend moved back in with her. I looked at this picture and chose to go back where I could get free drugs. Yes, I went back to the same rotten boyfriend who physically abused me. It wasn't like I had better choices. The drug habit was worse than before. One night, I was at my boyfriend's house and I started crying and told him I wanted help because I couldn't go on living like this. Then he said, *"Come on. Where do you want me to take you?"* I told him that I wanted to go to the hospital so that I could get to a detox program. I needed to go where there was a walk-in facility. While we were on our way in the car, I changed the radio station. Why did I do that? All of a sudden, he backhanded me and my mouth started to bleed. He stopped at a light, and I began to jump out of the car. He tried to hold onto me, but in the tussle, I came out of my coat, leaving it behind, and ran down the street. It was bitter cold, but I just kept running for about four blocks. All of a sudden, I heard a voice say, *"Miss, are you alright?"* I would not look; I just kept walking. Then this person shined a light in my face and I looked up. It was that same policeman! I went to his car and asked him and his partner to take me to the hospital so I could get help for myself. They agreed, but not without a lecture before I got out of the car.

I stayed in detox in the hospital for seven days before a rehabilitation center was found for me to enroll in. Although a center was finally located, I was told that I had to wait seven days before I could go there. In the meantime, I had to leave the detox center because the policy stated that after seven days, a patient must be discharged from the program. I didn't want to go home and pleaded for them to keep me in the program. But, the policy had to be adhered to; plus, the bed was needed for someone else. When I got home, I called every rehab I could think of, but there were no vacancies in any of them. I was desperate for help and saw the lack of available rehabs as another "rejection." A reject that I could not handle! So, instead of waiting the seven days to go to the rehabilitation center that the detox program located, I got high that night; and, it was back to business as usual!

THIRD CHILD BORN

•

DEATH OF SISTER

•

DEATH OF TWO BROTHERS

•

DEATH OF FATHER

I moved in with my sister and her husband and later found out that I was pregnant with my third child. We argued and fought every night. I was between a rock and a hard place. I really wanted to stop getting high, but I could not. I had my son with me. My older sister got saved and my mother went back to church. I started working for some perfume company. I worked the late shift, 3-11 pm, and was working in the bar on weekends. I smoked up all that money every week and did not have money to get to work when I did go. I fell and broke my leg and was given a settlement of $5,000.00. I smoked until all money was gone. Everything I got my hands on I would spend on drugs. That pipe was calling me and I answered every time. The devil was trying to take me out, but God had His hand on me. He was keeping me for a reason. I know this now.

My sister went to church with my mother and she ministered to my other sister and she also got saved. That's when my family began to turn around. My sister was delivered from heroine. Another sister was delivered from cocaine. When I think back on it, I used to ask her to stay when she came to visit every once in a while. I knew she would protect me. But, she would leave the next morning. My mother would usually say something to make her mad. If I knew someone really loved me, it was my sister. She looked out for me and defended me.

My oldest sister invited me and my son to come live with her. She was a praying woman. About a month after we moved in, she got sick and went into the hospital. The prognosis was poor; my sister was told she had full-blown AIDS.

She was given one month to live, but God kept her. One day she asked me if I wanted to know the Lord. I told her I was not ready. I would be asleep on the couch and would feel her hand anointing my forehead with oil. When I would get up and ask her what she was putting on my forehead, she'd laugh and say "blessed oil!" She told me I was going to be someone great in God one day. She used to speak life over me, even though I was killing myself with drugs. By then, I was smoking crack so bad that my 150-pound body was reduced to weighing just *70 pounds!* I was really in a bad shape, but I couldn't break my drug habit. I would go out, but not stay out all night. I wanted my sister to think I wasn't getting high any more. But she knew I was still doing drugs; I was only fooling myself. One day, I went out and when I came back my sister was in so much pain that she asked me – a drug addict – *"Do you know how to pray? Please ask God to stop the pain."* My son was asleep on her bed; she loved that little boy. She used to call him "baldy" because he never had any hair. I did ask God to stop the pain my sister was feeling and to heal her. That was the first healing prayer I ever prayed.

Soon after, I found an apartment for me and my son. Even after we moved in, I would bring him to my mother's house on the weekend so he could go to church, and

I would get high. Then one day, we got a call from the morgue to claim my brother's body. Cause of death: AIDS. I was so broken over his death. My father came home to my mother with lung cancer. I must say, my mother took care of him until he died. A lot of women would not have done this, being he left her with eight children to raise alone. I was in the dark about many things until my mother told us the truth after he died: my father had left us for another man. As though these tragedies were not enough, my oldest brother died in North Carolina from alcohol poisoning. God wasn't just speaking to our family, He was sounding a blaring alarm! My sister who God kept even when the doctors said she will not live passed a month. Lived almost two years, then she passed from Aids.

WAKE-UP CALL

At this point, I had had enough! It was time for me to get my life together. All my sisters and brothers were dying; and, I refused to go out like that. One New Year's Eve, my son said to me, *"Mom, come and go to church with me."* I told him no and he said, *"God loves you."* All my friends got scared when he said that. Even though they were users like me, they told me he was being used by God. They had sense enough to see God in my son's life. Then the doorbell rang. It was my daughter coming to wish me a Happy New Year. She would stop in from time to time and ask me if I was tired yet.

That particular night when I was getting high with my home girls, I heard the Lord speak to me and tell me if I hit that pipe, I would die. This time, I took heed, put down the pipe, and asked my friends to get down on their knees and pray with me. Of course, they would not. I didn't know what to say, so I asked God to take the taste of drugs from me. Believe it or not, I stopped getting high the next day. My sister and her girlfriend took me to detox in 1995. This time, they found a rehab for me where I was admitted. I spent two years there. I worked at night and I went to group sessions during the day. My girlfriends who were in my house had died. One died of AIDS and the other died from getting high. Her body just couldn't handle the poisons any longer. I am certain that I would have died with them, but I asked God to remove the taste of drugs out of my mouth and He did. That's when I knew the power of prayer was real. It really does work.

I was released from the rehabilitation center in 1997 and went to a shelter for one week. Then, I went to a transitional housing facility. I went back to get my children, but my daughter didn't want to come with me. She would turn eighteen in a week, so I didn't force her. My oldest son, who had been raised by my mother, was now in college. I got my youngest son, who was just 13 years old and also living with my mother. I had asked her to keep him until I came out of the rehab center. He and I were now going to make a go of life together.

SAVED!

I moved in transitional housing with my son. At the Transitional housing I met a Pastor who was mentoring the women at the facility. They use to ring the bell for church services. We would go in the lobby and they would have a church service in the library. I got saved and I started going to the Church and God began to deal with me I was still sleeping with my boyfriend who use to beat me up. I went over his house one Friday and the lord spoke to me and said (get up put your clothes on you are a child of God and you better not go back there any more). From that day on I was Holy and scared that God was going to get me. But my Pastor began to teach on how we should live, and the Word of God said you should treat your body like a living Sacrifice Holy unto God.

Then two Months Later my life change. My daughter's father died from alcohol poisoning. We buried him, and I did not cry one time, I often wonder why. Now I know God had delivered me from him. Because there was a (soul-tide) that was keeping us together so God had to cut it. One day one of our Pastors taught on it he said every thing you own that is from that boyfriend, get rid of it!!!! I went home and got rid of the stuff I took from his house and through it all away. That man was coming to me from the grave and God broke that (soul –tide). My baby son went to college that year to god be the Glory!!!!!!!!

I been at the Church every since, I never forget the first day I came to the Church, I met my Pastor baby daughter she said (my name is…and you)? are and I told her my name and my son's name. She took me and my son over to meet her mother. She was so nice after being at the Church for almost twelve years she has never changed. I joined the Church when I heard Pastor preach he made me feel like there was hope for my life, I sat under his teaching and I began to apply the Word to my life one day he (said; it was favor in the house.) He said; (go to the dealer ship and get a new car), (go to the bank and get a mortgage). So I got up the next day went to the bank and I told the bank representative I said my Pastor said God was giving me a new house, low and behold I got the Mortgage.

FINANCIAL CHANGES

•

NEW HOME

I got a new job making thirty thousand a year, I just was so happy my life was going to turn around. I started working outreach for the Church part time. That's where I met a very good friend who became my best friend. She had lost her husband and I took that time to lend an ear to her. I just let her talk and I just listen. I felt like I knew her husband, it was helping her when she talks about him. She is a very wise woman she is full of compassion and love for people. She tells me when I am wrong and she tells me if I am right.

One night she said lets go by and see the town houses the church had built. I told her one of those town houses was suppose to be mind. She said one of them is back up for sell she said go claim your town house. I remember my Pastor preaching about (every where your feet shall tread shall be yours.) I got out the car and I walked on the land I did this for a week every night we would stop by their and walk on the land, I heard god say (it's yours.).

Then about a week later we were coming in from work to punch out and the head of the program said Geneva I been looking for you. You are next on the list for that town house the people who was going to buy it has rescinded on it. The first time they said I did not make enough money for the town house. This time I made enough money to apply for the house. The part time work

I was doing at the church put me in the range I needed to be in.

Some one else at the church was applying for the town house they said who ever gets the mortgage first would be eligible. I got it and now I was looking for closing money and my friend gave me a check for the money I needed to close. On closing day I was on my way to closing and the trains coming out of New York was delayed because the signal light was broken. I stayed at the train station for three hours trying to get a train. Every body I called never picked up their phone. I kept calling my attorney office to tell her what was going on. Finally got my friend who came out of the doctor's office and called me back. She took me to closing and every thing went well they waited for me and we closed.

So many obstacles but God won in the end, when you are going through remember you are on the winning side if you are on God's side. I was a home owner!!!!!!! To God is the Glory!!!!!!!! I was so excited I slept on the floor of my new home the day I close.

The movers could not move my furnishing until the next morning. I walk through my new home thanking God for all he has done for me. I cried all night long, for the first time I had tears of joy.

Well it's time for a house blessing I called the church and got Pastor schedule. That day of the house blessing I was running around the house Pastor is coming to my house?!! I was so excited!!!! I was so over whelm, because it was like out a fairy tale that this amazing man of God is taking time out of his busy schedule to come to my house. I was so nervous; when he came in I could not say anything but nod my head. He began blessing the house on the first floor. When he started walking up the stairs he said you have people here I said yes just some of your staff. When he finish he sat down and had refreshment. I was so blessed on that day I will never forget it because I am going to get another house and I hope he would do me the honors of blessing it.

NEW HEALTHY RELATIONSHIPS

Finally I can have a little of peace in my life, no matter what happen I will continue to serve the Lord. I had to tell my self that every day because my life was filled with a lot of disappointment, and despair, anger, and lost, hope, fear, now I have Peace, I began to trust Love and form healthy relationship with people and trying to form them with my family. That's when I met another close friend and her husband.

One night she took me home from church and she said she never saw the inside of the townhouses. So I invited her in, as we began to go to the third floor I looked back and she was crying. I turned and I said what the matter is, she said she was so happy to see god's hand at work. I never saw some one so happy for me and she had just met me. We are known for the dynamite duel when it comes to decorating for affairs. My First lady gave us that name.

When ever I go to her and her husband they always listen and they tell me when I am acting ugly. They are always behind me and there for any thing I do. If I say I want to go back to school they say do it. They are real encouraging Saints and they are real saints.

These are just a couple of the people who I form healthy relationships with. Then there is Mother B was like a mother to me. Some times God put people in your life to help you through your heart ache and pain. I remember when I was going through some changes with my family, and I was going on and on and she said I do not see any blood yet. What she meant was get over it you are not bleeding if you was beat like Jesus was on that cross. So this is small so get over it and turn the page. We need people to take us out of our pity party with tough love. I have met the good the bad and the ugly since I have been save but I have seen more good.

(To God Be the Glory)!!!!!! I just met a new friend about a year now. With her what you see is what you get; she is one of the transparent persons I ever met. She is God sent her motto is never let them see you sweat. She can take something bad and bring good out of it; she will have you, feeling so good you will forget the bad that were done to you.

We need more people like her in this world. She got me looking at things that come to me I have to face I look for the good in it. If I can't I count it a lesson to be learn.

GOD'S KEEPING POWER

I lost my job and I started to get in financial trouble. I stayed in my house for four years, and then I lost it. But waiting for God to show up and he didn't I was devastated. But God kept my mind and brought me through another trial and he kept me.

The devil was telling me to go back to drugs because nothing was going to get better. I would, however, go to church anyway. Once, I got into an incident with one of our church leaders. Then some of the other leaders began treating me like I was the plague. I made a mistake and said something I should not have said. The consequences were heavy; I paid dearly for that remark. Nevertheless, I wondered why everyone was treating me like this. I went to church and felt like I was alone. I felt like I did not belong. There was a war going on inside of me. I was torn between staying with God and going back to the streets. I would wait for the point in the service called the "hug of love". This is where we greeted first-time visitors and one another. The "hug of love" was the only hug I was going to get for the week. Sometimes just that hug gave me hope to go on. It made me feel that someone cares.

Depression was very deep in my life at that time. A storm was brewing and about to erupt on the inside. There were days I felt like I was in a dark pit and could not get out. My mind was somewhere else. It was wandering into the past and back again. I started thinking about how I could give myself an extra shot of my insulin and end my life. But then, I took a look back over my life and I declared that the devil was and is a liar. I began to remind that same devil that when I needed somewhere to stay, God provided. When I wanted to come off the drugs, God provided. When I asked Him for my children *and* their forgiveness, God provided. When I asked Him for a house, God provided. When I asked Him for money to close on the townhouse, He provided. The more I thought, the more I realized that I *had* to stay with God and keep living! End of story.

I know that the Word says in Philippians chapter 4, verse 19 "but my God shall supply all your need according to His riches in glory by Christ Jesus." I believe this; I believe that God will handle all my needs. There are several other scriptures that anchored my faith:

"I have never seen the righteous forsaken nor His seed begging bread."

(Psalm 37:25)

"Trust in Him with all your heart and don't lean toward your own understanding."

(Proverbs 3:5, 6)

"Resist the devil and he will flee from you."

(James 4:7)

When you quote the Word of God, the enemy just cannot stand it! I kept rehearsing God's word out loud to the darkness that was trying to close in on me and make me doubt my God. I'm here to tell you – or better yet *WARN YOU* – not to go back to those places God has brought you from. It's as bad as returning to your own vomit. (Proverbs 26:11) I know without a doubt, that "if it had not been for the Lord on my side, where would I be?" (Psalm 124:1-2)

I struggle every day with my addiction, but I don't let it consume me. I stay in the word of God and I stay on my knees. If you want to be kept, I am a witness that God will keep you. Every day I wake up, I see new mercies straight from the hand of God. I have not yet "arrived," but I know I am holding onto God's unchanging hand. He kept me in the midst of so very much trouble and I owe God. I cannot repay Him enough.

Those of you who may be coming through an addiction of any nature, let me caution you that you cannot hang out with the people you used to hang out with because sooner or later, you will be back to your old destructive habits. I had a minister tell me once, *"Oh girl, you'll be alright. Come on and go out with us tonight and we'll have a glass of wine and a comedy show. You'll be fine."*

I said to her, *"First of all, I know a glass of wine will make me want a Bacardi and Coke. From there, I'll be back out in the streets looking for cocaine. I know I cannot drink any alcohol because it's a trigger for me that will lead me right back to drugs. I hope you won't invite anybody else that's a recovering drug addict out for wine. What about that oath you took when you became a minister? I don't drink, don't intend to, and you shouldn't either! If you do drink, please don't try to bring someone else into what you're doing. Truth be told, you know it's wrong. If I wasn't grounded in the Lord, you could have sent me back out in the streets!"*

I boldly walked away from this woman. I was angry, but I went home and I prayed for her. God kept my mind and brought me through yet another trial. Sometimes temptation can find you even in the church, but it's up to you how you respond.

MOVING DAY: PRESSURE IS ON

I started looking for somewhere to live. My family did not have room for me. My mother was afraid of losing her Section 8 privileges if I were to stay with her. I thought to myself, *"Here we go again, the same revolving door."* I had no place to go. This time, however, I had the Lord on my side. I asked God to help me and He did. One of my friends from church told me her friend had just bought a house and was looking for someone to rent a room. I got the room the day before they came to lock the door to my townhouse. Even then, God was making ways for me to have somewhere to lay my head. As God would have it, I moved in the room on the same day they padlocked my townhouse; and, I found a job in a restaurant earning only seven dollars an hour. I asked God, *"Where are you?"*

I went to the hospital only to discover my glucose levels were out of whack. I was not making it any better by taking a train and two buses to work in Newark, plus a cab to get back home at 2 o'clock in the morning. Once again, things were beginning to look bleak. Although I was only renting a room, I didn't make enough money to pay my rent. Most of the money I earned was spent on transportation. Because I couldn't pay the rent on the room, I was asked to move. I did not know what I was going to do. Shortly after that, my mother had congestive heart failure twice in one month, and my son dropped out of school. He had some tickets he hadn't paid and was caught driving without a license and no seat belt. I had my furniture in storage, but could not pay the bill. Eventually, those things went to auction and I lost everything I owned. I was devastated. I felt like I was losing my mind, but I kept on reading a particular healing scripture that our pastor had given us one Sunday. (Psalm 118-17) " I will not die but live to tell what the Lord has done." God's word kept me in the midst of all this turmoil.

I went to the Social Security psychiatrist and he said my mind was operating at only a capacity of ten percent. He then declared that I was disabled. He also said that I was not functioning as a person in their right mind. Nevertheless, GOD KEPT ME! God's Word overrode what the doctor said, as well as what I felt. I realized that "God had not given me a spirit of fear but of love, power, and a sound mind." (II Timothy 1:7) I did not take any medication because the Lord kept me functioning with my mental faculties intact. In the natural, I was diagnosed as being "crazy." In the Spirit, however, God had my mind and my whole being in His care. He promised that He would never leave me or forsake me. God does not break His promises.

You know, when I look back at that time in my life, I realize that no one held me together except God!!! I was operating on only two or three hours of sleep each night. I couldn't sleep; I was just too stressed out.

When I moved out of the room I was renting, I came to the conclusion that I had to throw my pride out the window. I went to the welfare office and they put me up in a homeless motel. I woke up with bed bugs biting me! Again, I asked God *"Where are you?"* He was real quiet.

There are times when God wants to see if you will praise Him in the midst of trying times. I went to church and I praised God like I had a gun to my head. Don't get me wrong, there were many days I wanted to give up. But when I thought about my children and my children's children, I got strength to go on. I have learned during my walk with God not to always question Him or attempt to figure Him out. It is best to go with the flow and let Him have His way. Quite frankly, I had no other option.

STARTING SCHOOL

When I laid in that hotel, I was a yielded vessel before God. I heard God tell me to go to school. Quite honestly, I wasn't prepared to deal with that at this point in my life. I often think about my other pastor who had a meeting with me about the "call" on my life. I told her that I never finished high school and that God had given me jobs for which I really didn't qualify. I thought I was telling her how blessed I was, until she responded *"What are you going to do about the fact that you don't have your diploma?"* I could not say anything. I was fearful about going back to school. God certainly used my pastor.

All I could think about when I left her office was our conversation. I had the nerve to get angry at first. I thought, *"Who does she think she is telling me to go back to school?"* Jesus did say that the truth will set you free… and it did! Even still, I started coming up with excuses. *"I can't go back to school with those kids, they will laugh at me! What if I fail?"* Nevertheless, I could not shake this idea. It had been birthed in my spirit from the time the Lord spoke to me in that infested motel room. It was then that I had a change of mind. My pastor's suggestion was really a confirming voice. I just wasn't ready to hear it again!

In spite of my fears, I went to the library and found all the material I could related to Adult Night School and I applied. I got my schedule in order, took two buses and my life as a student began even though I was old enough to be my classmates' mother! I know God directs everything I do. He was the one doing this, not me.

On many days, it was a challenge for me. I was dealing with depression and diabetes. Both were trying to stop me from going, but each day, I got up, pressed my way, and went to school. I only missed one day, and that was because school was closed! I had to do 9th, 10th, 11th and 12th grade work. But it didn't matter. I was not aiming for a GED; I wanted a real high school diploma.

I completed this coursework in two years. I had four condensed years of Math, English, Reading, and two years of Science and History. I also took Shop and Computers. I was convinced of what the Bible says in Philippians 4:13, *"I can do all things through Christ who gives me strength."* I have the mind of Christ to overcome anything. My completion of high school at age 53 is proof positive of that!

GRADUATION DAY

•

FAMILY STRESSES

On June 14, 2008 – my graduation day –my family stated they were busy and could not attend the ceremony, not even my children. I was upset and disappointed. I wondered when they would forgive me for my past. I think about it often. Since God has transformed my life, I now realize how important it is to stand behind and support your family.

When I arrived at the school, I was very quiet. We were escorted to a room to put on our robes. My mind began to flash back to the principal who called me in and told me that I had to remove the word God from my speech. I told her I could not do it; I refused to compromise. I could not represent our graduating class without honoring God. She gave the speech to another student. But, I didn't care. All I want to do in life is to please God, not myself.

When the class began to march in, I did not see anyone in the audience cheering for me. The tears began to roll down my cheek. I wiped my face quickly because I didn't want anyone to see me cry. The ceremony started early for some reason, so I started focusing on the program. I looked at it for a while as I listened to the speaker who did the welcome address. I happened to look up and I saw my pastor's wife coming in the door. Behind her were one of our elders, a minister, and three deacons coming through the door. Then I saw three more of my church family members and friends. I threw my hands up and said quietly, *"Thank you, Jesus!"* God had sent my family after all; He sent my church family! I love my biological family very much and am looking forward to the day when we will be reconciled to one another. But, I thank God that I can always rely on Him to always send my church family when my natural family does not respond. I thank God for giving me a church family that I can spend holidays with so I don't have to be alone.

I love my family very much and I am sorry for what happened in the past. I'm sorry for the pain I caused, and for the pain that we caused each other. But, God has removed the guilt that I carried for so many years and have replaced it with the assurance that one day we will be reconciled as a family in love and in peace. This is my prayer; God is faithful and I look forward to that day. In the meantime, I must press on; on toward the mark of the high calling in Christ Jesus! (Genesis 19-26) I will not be like Lot's wife in the Bible. She disobeyed the command of God, looked back and turned into a pillar of salt. I have to run on to see what the end is going to be. I stand today with a high school diploma! To God be the glory! I have this confidence in God that my future is very bright.

Shortly after graduation, I was accepted into Kean University. I declared a major in Criminal Justice. I have just completed my second year at Kean with a 3.70 GPA in 2009. Once again, TO GOD BE THE GLORY!!!

I do not have everything all figured out by any means, but I do know I am not going to give up. I like what God is doing in my life. For the first time in my life, I LOVE ME! I am a changed, blessed, and highly favored woman! I can look at myself in the mirror and smile at the person I see. I finally believe the words of Jesus that *"with God, all things are possible to them who believe."*

So, as I continue this fight and this journey to go all the way with God, pray for me. I will be praying for this whole world to come to know Jesus Christ and be saved and have the freedom that only He can give.

ABOUT THE AUTHOR

Geneva Evans was born and grew up in the city of Newark, New Jersey. For twenty five years her life spiraled out of control because of drug abuse. Determined to turn her life around, Geneva turned back to God and through prayer, strength and sheer determination, she conquered the demon of drug addiction. Geneva has been clean and sober for the past fifteen years.

Having a yearning for education, Geneva went back to school and earned her High School Diploma on June 11, 2008. After this success, her yearning for higher learning grew stronger. And in September 2008, after being accepted into Kean University in Union, New Jersey, she began working to earn a degree in Criminal Justice. During the past two years of college, she has maintained a 3,70 GPA.

Geneva has been a member of the Cathedral International in Perth Amboy, New Jersey for the past 13years under the leadership of Donald Hilliard, II. Presently, she serves as Ministry Leader of the Church's Encouragement Support Group. This group ministers to residents of halfway houses in the Central New Jersey area, sharing hope and offering strength to abuse women. They additionally visit group homes and minister to trouble teens who reside in these difficult settings. Geneva effortless gives back to all who needs to be encouraged. Her motto states, "An encouraging word can be the step to keep someone from giving up on life." Other church work includes singing with the choir during Sunday Morning Worship and serving as an Intercessory Prayer Warrior.

Geneva is the proud mother of three adult children, Calvin, Kisha and Terrance. She says, "I Love them with all my heart-they are my pride and joy.

Geneva has a wealth of expertise and wise counsel to offer women who have been physically, sexually, emotionally and verbally abused. With God's help, she will unquestionably attain her dream to complete college And become a full time advocate for abused women. As a women of God, she truly say that "Although my past was not good, my latter shall be so much greater."

Resources
(Hot Line)

National Domestic Hotline
1800-799-SAFE

National Sexual Assault
1800-856-HOPE

ROSE FUND
Help you regain your self esteem
Reconstructive Surgery
Scholarship Program
info@rosefund.org
Phone- 1- 617-482-5400

The ROSE Fund
200 Harvard Mill Square
Suite 310
Wakefield, Ma 01880

Drug & Alcohol
National Institute of Drug and Alcohol Abuse
1-301 443-1124
http://www.drugabuse.gov/

Notes

Notes

Notes

Notes

Notes

Notes

Notes